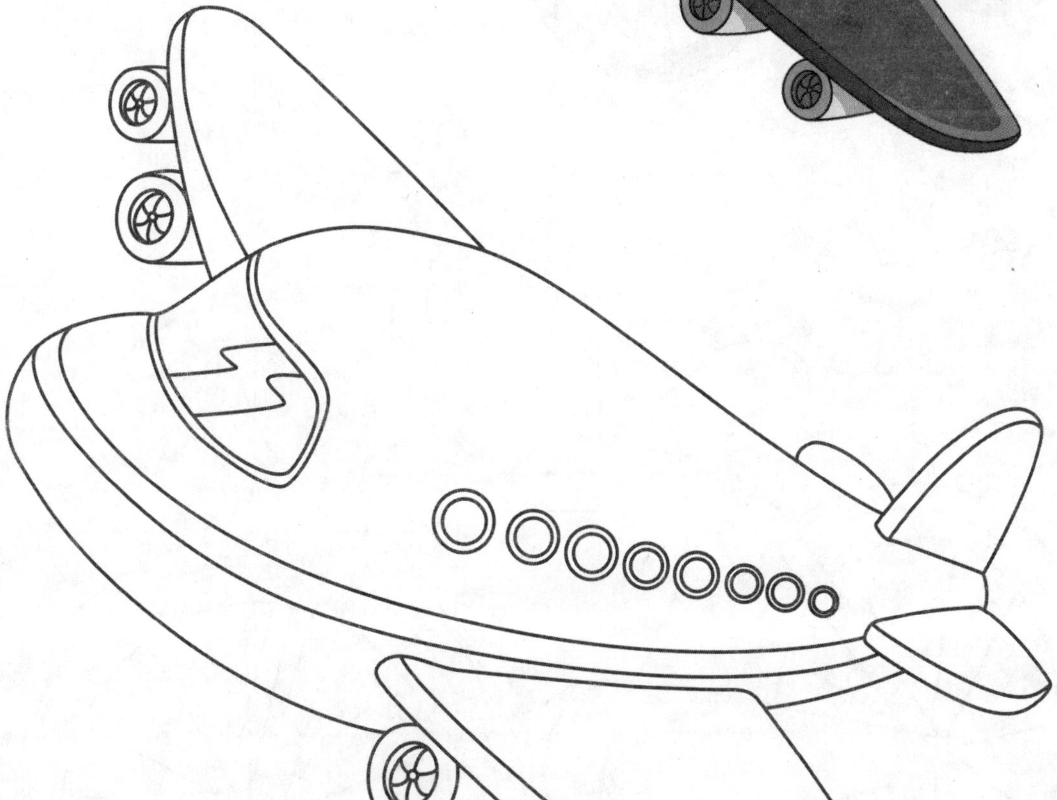

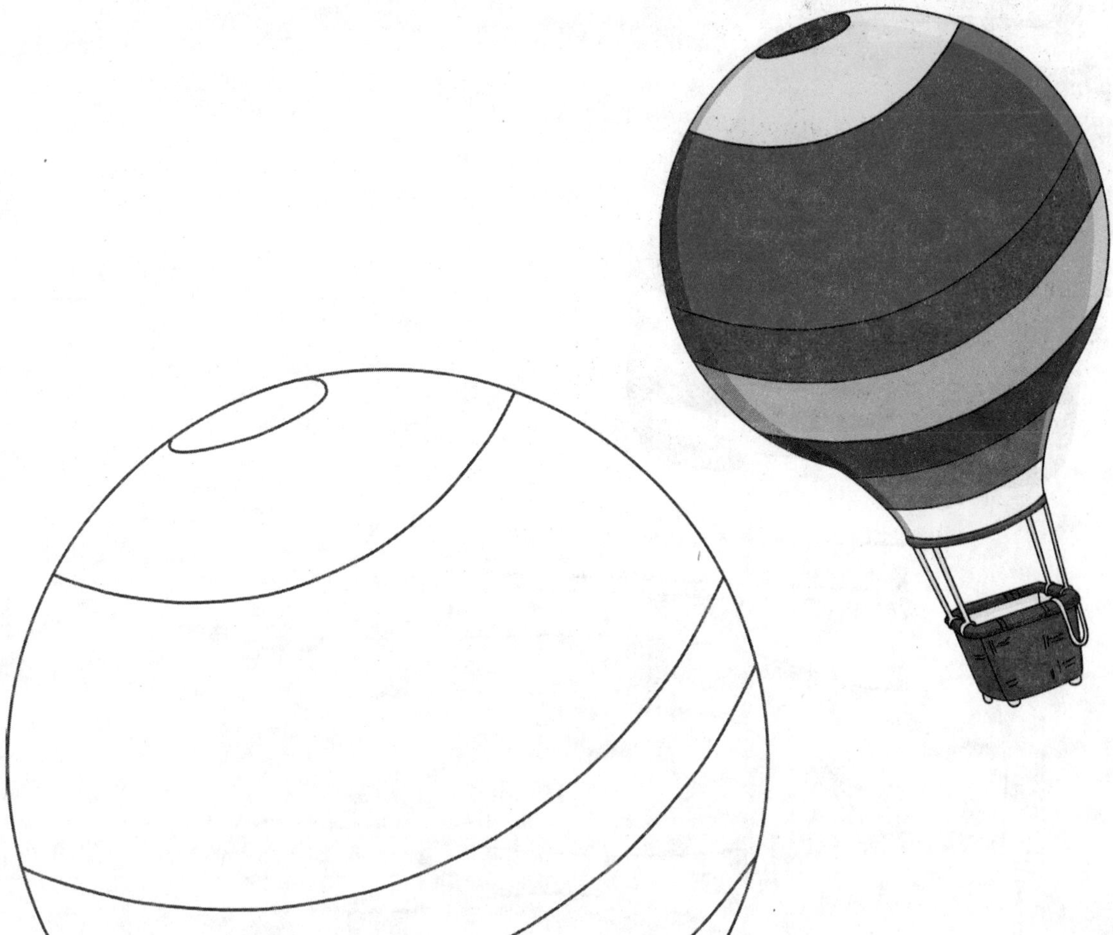

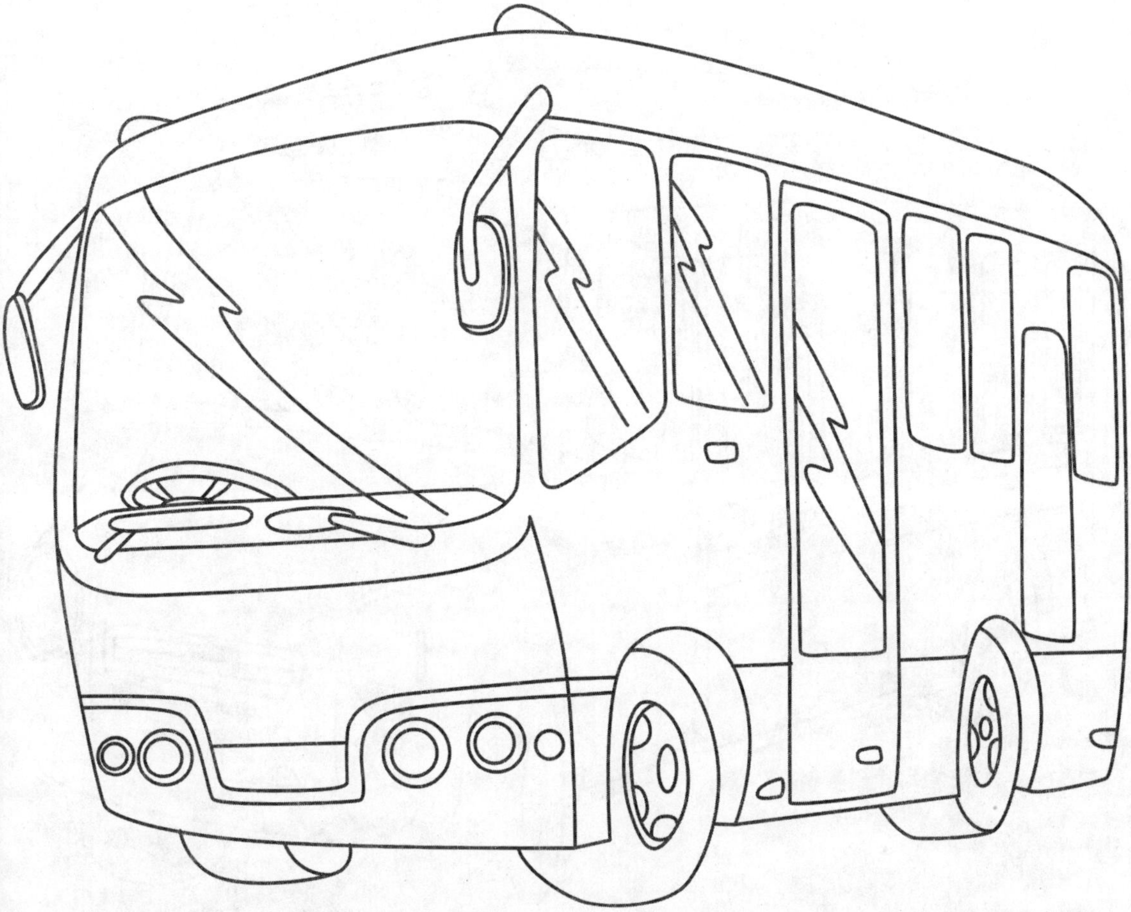

SCHOOL BUS

SCHOOL BUS

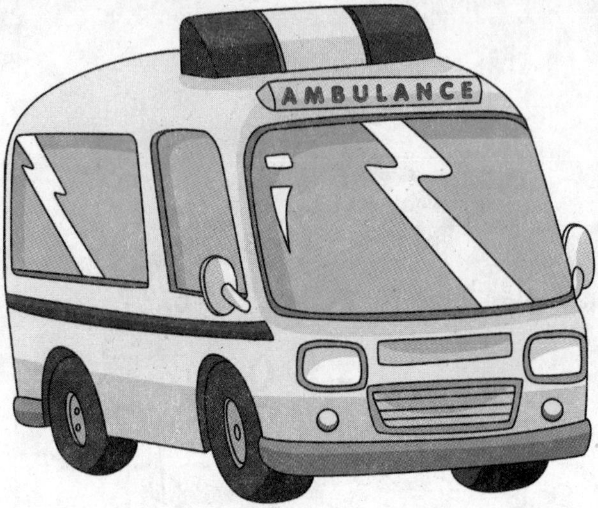
AMBULANCE

AMBULANCE

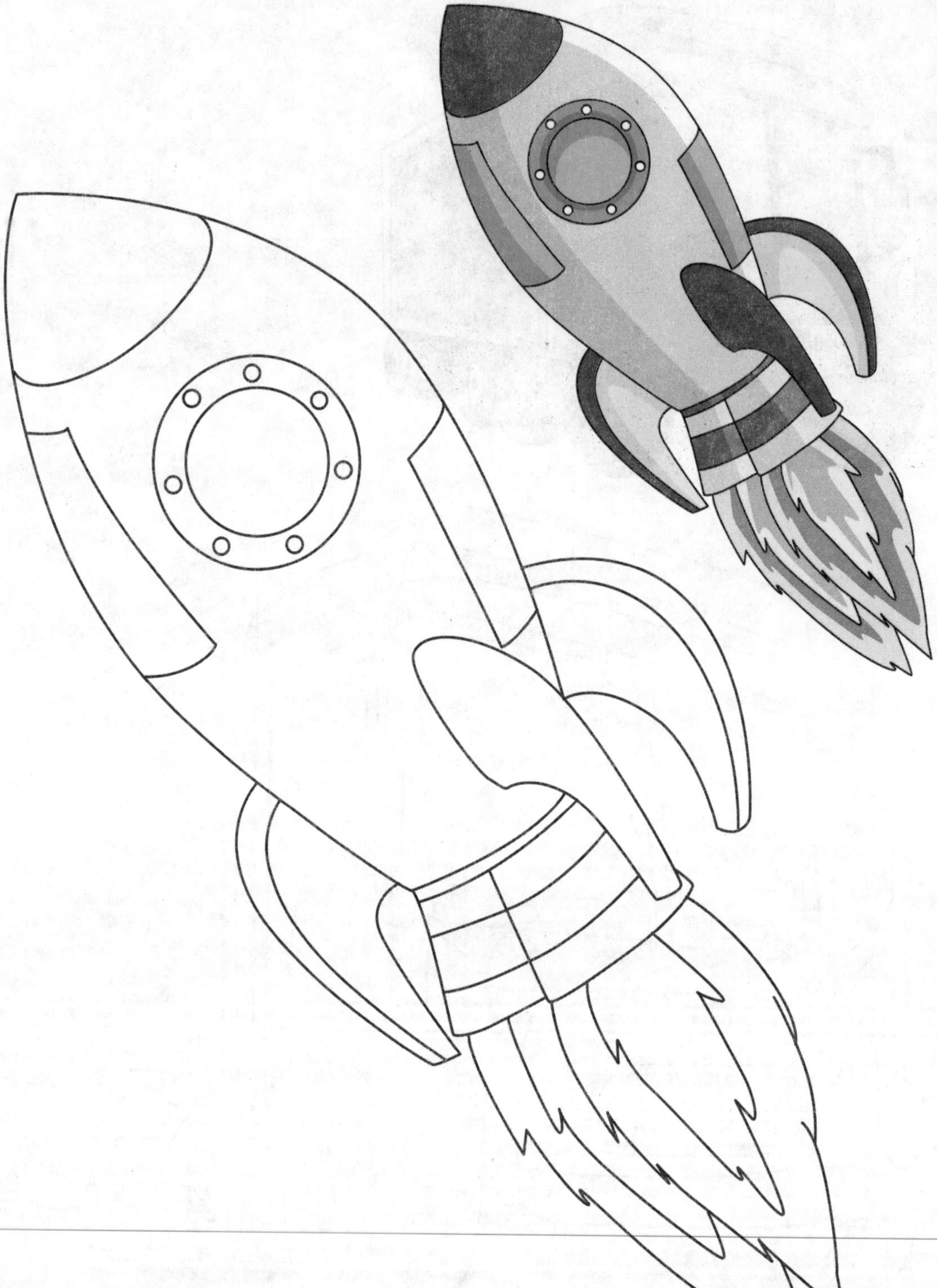